Olix S

Funny Bunny

Happy coloring pages

I0425645

This book with unique illustrations of cute rabbits and Easter Holiday pictures decorated with fancy floral patterns. The drawings are created according to the anatomic animal shapes with ornate original patterns. Fantasy picture for creative coloring, for any age. Be inspired by these funny stories of bunny and to convert black and white illustrations into bright pictures.
Make it happy moments. Good luck!

ISBN:9781096329015

www.ingramcontent.com/pod-product-compliance
Lightning Source LLC
Chambersburg PA
CBHW081421280526
45788CB00009B/3184